HMS SUPERB

By

Patrick Boniface

First published in 2006 by
Periscope Publishing Ltd
33 Barwis Terrace
Penzance
Cornwall TR18 2AW

A CIP record for this book is available from the British Library

ISBN No 1-904381-34-0

Printed by Antony Rowe Ltd. Eastbourne

TABLE OF CONTENTS

LIST OF ILLUSTRATIONS

Chapter 1

FORMER SUPERBS

HMS *Superb* ranks amongst the most illustrious names to have been carried by any ship in the Royal Navy, returning in no less than nine incarnations since 1710 and certainly living up to her motto

'With Sword and Courage'

According to Royal Navy records the first warship to bear the name ***Superb*** was a vessel taken from the French. The '***Superbe***' was a 4th rate of 56 guns was captured by HMS ***Kent*** and commissioned into the Royal Navy on 23 September 1710 as ***Superb***. This warship served with distinction with the Royal Navy throughout Queen Anne's War and also garnered a battle honour for the name when she participated in the destruction of the Spanish Fleet off Cape Passero on 31 July 1718. This vessel was decommissioned but then taken in hand for a major reconstruction that gave her new guns and a higher displacement. Thus she also became the second ship to bear the name ***Superb***. As such she would continue to serve in the Mediterranean and was also present at the capture of Louisbourg in June 1745.

The third ***Superb*** was a 3rd rate sailing ship built at Deptford in 1760 and having an armament of 74 guns. *Superb* was to have an illustrious career with numerous skirmishes with the French fleet mostly in the East Indies. One such occurred off Sadras, when with the *Exeter Superb* suffered severe damage and 11 killed including her captain William Stevens and 13 wounded. This tally would pale into insignificance later when off Cuddalore the *Superb* suffered 59 killed and 96 men wounded.

Superb would end her days on 5 November 1783 when she was wrecked off Tellichery without loss of life.

The next *Superb* was another captured French vessel *Superbe,* a corvette of 22 guns was taken by the *Vanguard* in September 1795. Within two years the ship had been sold out of Royal Navy commission.

Next in line was a warship built on the Thames in 1798. As designed *Superb* had 74 guns and had a displacement of 1927 tons. She was rated as a 3rd rate warship of the line. After commissioning the ship would eventually go on to serve the Royal Navy for twenty-eight years throughout some of the bitterest fighting of the Napoleonic Wars.

More than any other *Superb* she added most to the illustrious name. Her score sheet was opened when she took part in Admiral Sir John Saumarez's action at Algerciras on 12 July 1801. She would add to this by taking part in the Battle of San Domingo on 5 February 1806 and the Battle of Copenhagen. In 1814 she saw action off North America taking part in the conflict of 1812. In August 1816 at the end of a successful career *Superb* took part in her last action when she bombarded Algiers, but not without the loss of 8 men killed and 84 wounded by return fire. *Superb* went to the breakers yard on 17 April 1826.

The next *Superb* was to mark the transition of the Royal Navy from the era of sail to the era of steam. This warship was to be a second rate vessel displacing 2589 tons and having 80 guns. Her hull was laid down at Pembroke in 1838 and seven years later she was completed and handed over to the Royal Navy. Although she never fired her guns in anger she served well in the Mediterranean and Home waters, but also provided bed space for the outbreak of Cholera during the Crimean War. *Superb* later was moored off Sheerness in 1858 to serve as a hospital ship. Eleven years later she was broken up.

The sixth *Superb* was to have been a Turkish warship the *Hamidieh,* but was purchased from the Turks on the stocks at Blackwell for £443,000. She had been launched in 1875 as a Central Battery Ironclad and had a displacement of 9170 tons. *Superb* mounted a single 11-inch turret with muzzle loading guns. Her steam turbines could generate enough motive power to move the ship at 14 knots.

Superb took part in the bombardment of Alexandria on 11 July 1882, during which she was hit by three shells that claimed one dead and 3 men seriously injured. She was refitted and modernised at Portsmouth between 1893 and 1896, and was sold out of the Navy in May 1906.

The name *Superb* was then allocated to a new battleship being constructed at Elswick and was launched on 6 February 1907. The warship was the second member of the Bellerophon class of 18,000 tons with an armament of ten 12-inch guns and capable of 20 knots on her steam turbine. *Superb* saw action at Jutland in 1916, after which she served with sister ship *Temeraire* in the Mediterranean in 1918. In 1919 she become a turret drill ship before paying off in 1920. Her last years were spent as a target before being sold on 12 December 1923 for breaking up.

The current *Superb* is a nuclear powered hunter killer submarine of the Swiftsure class and was constructed by Vickers at Barrow in Furness. The submarine was laid down on 16 March 1973 and launched on 30 November 1974. Another two years of fitting out and trials saw her accepted into service with the Royal Navy in 1976. Since then the submarine has served in all oceans around the globe and went to war in the South Atlantic during the Falklands War of 1982, when she was shadowing Argentine warships. Since her entry into service the *Superb* has been upgraded frequently and will continue in service until 2008.

Chapter 2

THE CRUISER SUPERB

The steel that would eventually be tempered and moulded to form the hull of the cruiser *Superb* were first laid down on 23 June1942 at the Wallsend shipyard of Swan Hunters. The shipyard workers made steady progress with her construction and saw the warship launched into the River Tyne on 31 August 1943. Ahead was another two years of construction work. *Superb* missed taking part in the Second World War and with the pressure for her construction slackening work on more pressing concerns took precedence. Captain William Geoffrey Robson DSO, DSC took command of the cruiser on 21 August 1945.

Captain William Robson was born in Ceylon in 1902 and joined the Royal Navy at the age of 13 in 1915 as a cadet at the Royal Naval College Osborne and later at Dartmouth. Having been appointed as a Midshipman he went onto serve in the battleship *Malaya* before spending the next fifteen years of his life associated with destroyers. His first command came in 1934 when he took command of *Rowena* and later between 1935 and 1936 of the *Wren*. In 1940 he was awarded a DSO. World War Two saw him in command of HMS *Kandahar* until 1941 when he joined the staff of combined operations for a year. 1941 also saw a bar being awarded for his DSO and also a DSC to his distinguished list of awards.

In 1942 he was appointed to command the 26th Destroyer Flotilla and in 1944 in command of HMS *Hardy* he was Captain of Coastal Forces (Nore). In 1945 he took command of the brand new cruiser *Superb* as she was being built.

Eventually *Superb* was completed on 16 November 1945 and was commissioned into Royal Navy service the following month. Having sailed to Chatham in December *Superb* completed to full complement at Chatham on 29 December 1945. She also took on the role of Flagship of the 2nd Cruiser Squadron. At 04.00 on 16 January 1946 *Superb* sailed for Portland to carry out Pitometer log trials over the West Looe measured mile. Having arrived at Plymouth later the same day the cruiser anchored in Plymouth Sound for the night.

With her trials completed at 11.30 on 18 January 1946 *Superb* sailed for Gibraltar with *Cheviot* and *Childers*. The 3 ships arrived at Gibraltar at 13.00 on 21 January 1946. The next day *Superb* sailed for Malta with the destroyers *Cheviot* and *Childers* in company.

Malta was approached from the Southwest on the forenoon of Friday 25 January. A mass air attack had been laid on. *Superb*'s crew defended the ship well during the simulated attack. The cruiser berthed at Marsaxlokk anchorage at 15.00. On finding an ex-enemy cruiser *Guiseppi Garibaldi* in one of the best berths in Grand Harbour, Captain Robson arranged for an exchange of berths on Saturday 26 January 1946.

On arrival at Malta Captain Robson called on Vice Admiral Malta, Sir Frederick Dalrymple-Hamilton, KCB, His excellency the Governor Lieutenant General Sir Edmund C.A Schreiber KCB, the General Officer Commanding Troops and the Chief of Staff to the C-in-C, Mediterranean Station, Rear Admiral H A Parker, CB, CBE. Sir Frederick and Lady Dalrymple-Hamilton were entertained to lunch on board.

It was originally intended to go to sea about three days a week during the working up period and to use the remaining three days for harbour training drills. On 9 February 1946 a guard of 25 ranks and the band was provided at the request of Captain (D) Malta for the turnover of HMS *Tanatside* to the Royal Hellenic Navy. Due to the cancellation of practice because of weather in the first week and having to remain in harbour for the week commencing 11 February 1946 to clear up defects full four day practice programme had to be carried out in the 2nd week. On two separate occasions during working up *Superb* took part in comprehensive day and night exercises with *Ocean*.

At 18.00 on Friday 1st March *Superb* proceeded out of Grand Harbour on passage to Greenock. Good weather was experienced for the first 24 hours, and cleaning and painting of the ship continued. On the night of 2 March 1946, however, a short sharp storm was encountered. Strong winds persisted to Gibraltar, arrival being an hour and a half late at 09.30 on 4 March.

Superb was given an anchor berth. No oiler had appeared and at 11.53 orders was received to shift berth to alongside the Signal Tower inside the harbour, which was completed by 14.30. Oiling was commenced immediately. After three days at Gibraltar, *Superb* left port at 18.00 on the return leg to the United Kingdom.

Early on 5 March 1946 the Commander in Chief Home Fleet's message stated that *Superb* would be required for further service on 8 April and that men due to be released before June 10 were to be relieved also, as much leave as practicable was to be granted. The necessary steps were therefore taken to apply for relief's and the captain proposed that one third of the ships company should be sent on leave on arrival for 12 days, thus not being on board for the passage to Belfast with HRH Princess Elizabeth. The passage to Greenock was made at 16 knots in good weather throughout arriving at 14.00 on 8 March 1946.

The period from 8 March – 18 March was spent in preparing the ship for passage to Belfast with HRH Princess Elizabeth and her staff, allowances were made for the possibility of one night having to be spent onboard in the event of bad weather. Repairs were carried out to the Quarterdeck Semtex and carpets were fitted in the after cabins.

HMS *Fame* (Commander J Grant DSO) and *Hotspur* (Lt Commander D R Mallinson) were escorts and had arrived at Greenock by 16 March. Opportunity was taken to practice berthing *Fame* alongside and adjusting the brow as necessary to transfer the Princess to *Fame* off the Pile Light at Belfast. This transfer was necessary because the arrival at Belfast was timed for 16.30 on 18 March one hour before low water equinoctial springs. The resident Naval Officer Belfast and the harbour authorities were anxious to take *Superb* straight up harbour at that time, but as the chart showed no more than 2 feet of water under the ships bottom the Captain of *Superb* disagreed.

All three ships embarked Belfast pilots on 17 March and the next day *Superb, Hotspur* and *Fame* were dressed overall when the Royal Train arrived at Princes Pier promptly at 09.50. The Navy ships looked smart and clean.

HRH Princess Elizabeth embarked at 10.00 and her standard was broken at the main, this being the first occasion on which it had been worn by one of HM ships. She inspected the Guard of Honour. Also with her were Admiral Sir William J Whitworth,

KCB, DSO, Commander in Chief Rosyth and his flag lieutenant. Captain Sir Harold Campbell, KCVO, DSO, ADC and the Princesses lady in waiting The Lady Mary Strachey plus representatives from the press. Once done the Princess went below, where the Captain's suite had been prepared for her.

HRH Princess Elizabeth came forward by the inside route on to the Compass Platform because the decks were wet and gave her permission to sail. Two chairs were available on the Compass Platform and HRH Princess Elizabeth and the Lady in Waiting took these for the passage down to the Cumbraes. Salutes were received from all warships and merchant ships as *Superb* passed.

After lunch HRH Princess Elizabeth returned to the bridge at 15.00 off the coast of Ireland. Thirty-five-minutes later the destroyer *Hotspur* detached. At 15.45 *Superb* anchored off Pile Light. *Fame* then berthed alongside at 16.00. First to leave the cruiser were representatives of the press who photographed and reported the Royal party's transfer at 16.20. As she left the ship, *Superb*'s crew manned ship and cheered the Princess.

When the tide was right to proceed up harbour, *Superb* did so at 20.00 on 18 March and berthed up harbour in Dufferin Dock No 3 berth. At 10.30 on 20 March *Superb* moved into the main stream turned and re-berthed bows out at Dufferin Dock in order to re-embark the Royal Party.

Superb's Commanding Officer and four officers were invited to the Governors Ball while 300 officers and men were invited to the launch of the aircraft carrier *Eagle* to control crowds. Having officially launched the Royal Navy's largest ever aircraft carrier, the Princess re-embarked at 10.50 on 21 March and *Superb* slipped and proceeded at 11.00 assisted by local tugs. The passage to Greenock was made in perfect weather conditions. HRH Princess Elizabeth was shown around the cruiser.

Upon reaching the Clyde approaches the three ships anchored in company and dressed overall at 16.30. *Superb* again manned and cheered ship when the Royal Barge left at 16.50. *Superb* shifted berth to D1 buoy at Sunset on 21st March and the first leave party was re-embarked.

On Monday 1 April she was still at Greenock and she remained there until the following Sunday when ***Superb*** slipped and proceeded to sea. Her ultimate destination was to be Gibraltar, where she arrived on Thursday 11 April at 06.25 in the morning. At Gibraltar the cruiser watched as the destroyer *St Kitts* and the submarine ***Truant*** left harbour. ***Superb's*** stay at Gibraltar was to be brief one because the next day she embarked some Army personnel as passengers for transportation to Malta. *Superb* slipped that day.

Upon her arrival at Grand Harbour in Malta on Monday 16 April *Superb* fired a salute to the Commander in Chief Mediterranean before securing to No 12 buoy. *Superb* would spend the next few weeks at Malta. On Tuesday 23 April the cruiser slipped at 09.00 and proceeded out of harbour and twenty minutes later she had passed the breakwater. Another ten minutes and the order were given to man ship and cheer Admiral Sir John Cunningham before taking up station astern of *Ajax*. *Superb* exercised with the cruisers *Ajax* and *Orion* and the destroyers *Volage* and *Virago* before returning to Marsaxlokk

More exercises followed over the next few days, but on Friday 26 April in company with *Orion Superb* set a course for Italy and the naval base at Trieste. En route to Italy on Sunday 28 April a reminder of the war in Mediterranean waters was sighted. A mine was located and shot at with rifles but this had no effect. *Superb* communicated the mine's position to headquarters who dispatched more suitable vessels to deal with the danger. The following day the two British cruisers arrived off Trieste and anchored offshore. A wonderful time was had by all at Trieste, but nothing compared with the scenery at Venice, which was next on the *Superb*'s itinerary. She arrived on Monday 6 May having only left Trieste a short time earlier. Only three days were spent at Venice before returning to Trieste and again onto Corfu.

On May 14th 1946 two British cruisers, *Orion* and *Superb* were on passage in the Corfu Channel, a narrow channel between the island of Corfu and the Greek mainland, a route regularly used by British warships steaming between the Mediterranean and the Adriatic. Mine clearance in the area was also a British responsibility, but due to the political climate at the time there was considerable anti-British feeling among the Albanians. An Albanian shore battery fired on the ships without any hits being scored, the British ships held their fire.

Naturally this brought a strong protest from the British Government who were not too thrilled at having their ships shot at. The diplomatic row between Albania and Britain ensued and only resulted in a series of weak excuses from President Hoxha of Albania. The British Government warned that if British ships were fired on again, then they would be ordered to return fire. The Albanians declared that all foreign ships would need permission to sail through the channel in International waters, Britain understandably rejected this out of hand.

In the afternoon of 22nd October 1946 the cruiser HMS *Mauritius* leading the destroyer *Saumarez,* followed by the cruiser *Leander* and another destroyer *Volage* were in the channel with guns trained fore and aft, but with orders to return fire if fired upon. The exercise was designed to show that ships could proceed safely in what were recognised as international waters.

During the passage down the charted swept channel a violent explosion occurred forward of *Saurmerez's* bridge as she hit a mine, followed by a fire. *Volage* took *Saurmerez* in tow but she hit a mine, which blew her bows off. Eventually all four ships returned to harbour, but there had been casualties, 44 men killed and 40 injured. *Saurmarez* was scrapped and *Volage* had a new bow fitted. The channel was immediately swept and the swept mines were found to be brand new and had not been in the water long.

Albania was taken to the International Court by Britain for illegally mining a swept channel and was found guilty and ordered to pay Britain £843,947 in damages, which have yet to be paid

On Wednesday 15 May 1946 *Superb* arrived at Corfu and was open to the public for part of the day including parties of Boy Scouts and Girl Guides. The following Wednesday *Superb's* cells were used to house Greek civilians accused of stealing. The men were put into protective custody in the early hours and remained there until local magistrates took them away at 10.10.

On Friday 24 May Superb left port just after three in the afternoon and made for Malta, where she arrived the next day and entered Grand Harbour. Five days of rest on Malta came to an end on 30 May when the cruiser was ordered to head towards Haifa where troubles had been brewing for some time. Soon after she had arrived *Superb* received threats from the Stern Gang, Israeli terrorists or freedom fighters. The threats boiled down to 'if *Superb* doesn't leave harbour we'll blow it up', so the ship did leave and the threat went away.

In June the problems off Haifa were concentrating the minds of British politicians and *Superb* was stationed off Israel. Having left Malta, *Superb* steamed for Haifa where she arrived on Monday 3 June, she would spend most of the following month there with members of her crew working in the town. On Saturday 22 June General Pileau joined the ship for passage back to the United Kingdom along with a number of other British passengers.

Superb put to sea the following day in mid afternoon and set a course for Malta. Three days later the cruiser eased into Grand Harbour and anchored. Only two days were spent at Malta before the journey back to Britain re-commenced and together with a brief stop at Gibraltar on Sunday 30 June she was back on 5 July. *Superb* arrived back at Chatham after her time in the Mediterranean. She was soon after attached to the 10th Cruiser Squadron.

July was spent at Chatham Dockyard and *Superb* only ventured to sea again on Thursday 15 August when she sailed for Portland. En route she exchanged messages with the destroyer *Solebay*. Portland was reached on Friday 18 August and as she entered the harbour already present included the battleship *Nelson* the cruiser *Diadem* and a host of other smaller vessels including *Opus, Seadevil, Scorcher, Oakum Castle, Tintagel Castle* and *St James*. The remainder of the month was spent at Portland.

On 1 September 1946 *Superb* was at sea in the English Channel and the following day arrived at Portsmouth and secured alongside the cruiser *Birmingham*. Two days later on Wednesday 4 September the flag of CS2 was transferred from *Birmingham* to *Superb* at 08.00 and ninety minutes later Rear Admiral Cunningham Grahame CBE boarded Superb.

The next day *Superb* slipped and headed for Portland to take part in exercises with *Escapade* and the submarine *Tudor* before finally arriving at Portland. The next five days were spent in Dorset before the cruiser sailed up the North Sea to Invergordon, where she would remain throughout the remainder of the month.

On Tuesday 1 October *Superb* was still at Invergordon and continued to exercise with units of the Home Fleet until mid month. On Wednesday 16th May the Commander in Chief Rear Admiral Parker joined the ship in full ceremonial attire to assume command from Rear Admiral Cunningham Grahame, who then left the ship. The following Monday *Superb* paid a visit to Golspie before once again heading back to the familiar surroundings of Invergordon.

On Wednesday 30 October *Superb* sailed south to Portland and en-route replenished at sea from the tanker RFA *Black Ranger*. On Saturday 2 November as the cruiser arrived at Portland at 11.45 and took station ahead of the battleship *King George V* before entering the harbour and securing to No 3 buoy at 14.02. Also in port at the time were the battleships *Nelson* and *Howe*, the frigates *Leeds Castle*, *Tintagel Castle*, the submarine *Tradewind* and the American cruiser USS *Spokane*. The next ten days were spent at Portland.

On Tuesday 12 November *Superb* set sail for an official visit to Antwerp in Belgium. The visit had been timed to coincide with the second anniversary of the re-opening of the port, since liberation from Nazi control. Onboard for the trip to Antwerp were two officers and six guardsmen of the 2nd Battalion of the Coldstream Guards.

After sailing from Portland *Superb* was the subject of mock torpedo attacks from Mosquito aircraft from Royal Naval Air Station Ford. The aircraft carried out numerous torpedo attacks whilst others strafed the ship.

Superb embarked a pilot at Flushing at 05.00 on Thursday 21 November and proceeded up harbour. At 09.30 she fired a National Salute of 21-guns. The Salute was returned from a battery at Fort St. Marie. An hour later she arrived at her berth and fired a series of salutes. Thirteen were fired for Mr E G Sebastian, His Majesty's Consul General, a further eleven were fired for Commodore Timmermans, Head of Belgian Naval Force.

On Friday 22 there was an official reception held onboard *Superb* for 120 guests. Later that evening, 13 officers and the Rear Admiral dined at Cercle la Concorde.

On Saturday 23rd at 11.30 members of the resistance were welcomed onboard. The members of the resistance were made to feel most welcome on board. Everyone agreed that the men and women were a fine collection of brave people. Before leaving the ship the resistance members presented the ship with an embroidered pennant to commemorate the visit. Later they gave a case of Bendictine to the cruiser's officers and later in the day members of the general public in Antwerp were invited to tour the British cruiser with great success. Less successful was a golf match laid on for members of the crew against Antwerp Golf Club, *Superb* lost the match, however honour was redeemed during a football match when *Superb* won 6-1.

On Monday 25 November in the morning 18 officers and ratings were taken to lunch and a visit to the Belgian Artillery School. Other visits were organised to the painter Reuben's House and the Rear Admiral laid a wreath on the tomb of the unknown Warrior in Brussels. A second football match in the afternoon resulted in defeat for *Superb* when they lost 2-3. At 16.40 the Royal Marines Band 'Beat the Retreat' in the Grande Place, Antwerp. Twenty minutes later in another part of the town, 30 members of the ships company were invited to tea by the Acting Burgomaster Monsieur Eekelers in L'Hotel de Ville.

Another mauling in sport followed the next day when *Superb* lost in both Golf and Football, but a more successful social occasion was a dinner party staged at 19.30. The guest list for the night included Monsieur Rongaux, Minister of Communications, the Governor of the Province of Flanders and Madam Declerck, The Acting Burgomaster and Madam Eekelers. Mr Preston the US Consul General and Mrs North, his sister. Finally Brigadier General Spears the Military Attache. During the dinner party the British film 'Blythe Spirit' was shown.

Another dinner party was staged the following day of the visit and this time the Rear Admiral invited onboard *Superb* the Belgian Prime Minister Camille Huysmans and his wife and Lady Knatchbull-Hugessen. At the second dinner party the question of the Royal Toast provided some difficulty. With the Belgian King in exile, a Prince Regent and a socialist Prime Minister, it had been intended on the advice of His Majesty's Ambassador to give the collective toast 'The King, the Regent and the Belgian Royal Family'. Rear

Admiral H A Parker instead deferred to the wishes of the Prime Minister and gave the toast 'The Head of the State'.

On the final day of the visit at 09.00 a contingent from the British cruiser together with a Belgian naval force attended a ceremony at the Mariners Memorial where the Rear Admiral laid a wreath. An hour later *Superb* slipped her moorings and after disembarking her pilot at Flushing started her journey back to Portland, where she arrived at lunchtime on Friday 29 November. *Superb* remained at Portland until Tuesday 10 December when she headed for her homeport of Chatham. By the next day she was secure within Chatham Dockyard and was alongside the 'farewell jetty' in Basin 3.

On 20 January 1947 *Superb* slipped from Chatham and proceeded up the River Medway past Sheerness and into the English Channel. She steered a course that would take her to Portland, where she arrived at 03.19 the next day. At 07.10 the cruiser *Dido,* which saluted the flag of Rear Admiral Parker CB onboard *Superb,* joined her. At 11.00 the crew of *Superb* exercised 'three cheers for their Majesties' and fired a salute.

On Wednesday 22 the oiler *Black Ranger* came alongside and oiled the cruiser as the battleships *Anson* and *Duke of York* entered Portland harbour and anchored some distance off. *Superb* remained at Portland until Saturday 1 February, when along with the Home Fleet centred on the battleships *Vanguard* and *Duke of York* she slipped to sea for Gibraltar. Again the ship's sides were lined and the crew cheered their Majesties. Destroyers from the 4th and 5th Destroyer Flotilla's screened the force.

On Wednesday 5 February *Superb* and *Dido* carried out a series of towing exercises before entering Gibraltar harbour via the Northern Entrance at 16.15. *Superb* tied up alongside 41 Berth with her bows facing south. Leave was granted to Blue and the 1st part of Stoker White Watch. The following Saturday the ship was open to visitors and many hundreds clambered around her upperworks. At 22.00 a small electrical fire was discovered in No 6 Power Room and was quickly put out.

Superb along with *Dido* and the destroyers *Myngs* and ***Dunkirk*** left Gibraltar on Wednesday 12 February for a passage to Casablanca at 17.55. The following morning at 07.53 ***Superb*** passed the cement works at Dar-El-Beida at 8 knots and a few minutes later picked up the local pilot. By 08.26 she fired a 21-gun salute before stopping her engines. Having been given clearance to proceed to her berth *Superb* entered through the harbour entrance and by 9.00 was alongside. From 3 o'clock in the afternoon the Admiral received a series of VIP visitors and each was accorded a gun salute. Rear Admiral Barset (13-guns), Brigadier General Capitant (13-guns), Monsieur Boniface (11-guns) and the *Pasha* of Casablanca (9-guns).

The following Saturday saw a dance ashore organised for the Chiefs and Petty Officers which saw the men dancing and drinking until the early hours. Meanwhile, the cruiser was once again open to the public, as it was on the Sunday of the visit.

At 10.00 in the morning of Thursday 20 February ***Superb*** slipped with the aid of local tugs and within a quarter of an hour had passed the breakwater, there she stopped briefly to disembark members of the press who had been onboard the ship. Once the journalists were safely on their way back to dry land, ***Superb*** quickly built up speed to 12 knots and resumed exercises with the ***Dido*** en-route to Gibraltar. The ships arrived back at Gibraltar on Saturday 22 February. Upon entering the harbour ***Superb*** was taken into No 1 Dock and by 10.00 had been handed over to dockyard control.

Superb remained in dock until Thursday 6 March when at 16.30 she was gently backed out of the dock with the assistance of local tugs. Ten minutes later with the same tugs she passed through the harbour entrance stern first. The local pilot was disembarked at 16.45 as ***Superb*** started the journey back to Portland. On Friday morning she spoke to the SS ***Robert Hill*** bound for Genoa and the following day closed to the battleship ***Duke of York***. ***Dido*** later joined the force and over the next few days all ships carried out a lengthy series of exercises. All the ships of the Home Fleet returned to Portland Harbour on Wednesday 12 March, with ***Superb*** passing the breakwater at 10.30 and securing to No 3 buoy. The following weekend saw strong winds gusting up to Force 8 in the harbour and the shackles keeping the cruiser to the buoy were checked regularly.

On Wednesday 19 March ***Superb*** left Portland at 07.21 for exercises during which the destroyer ***Zest*** came alongside to oil. ***Superb*** returned to Portland later the same day. She remained at the Dorset port until sailing for her homeport of Chatham on Tuesday 25 March. The River Medway was misty when she arrived the next morning and by 17.30 that afternoon she had been secured port side to the cruiser ***Achilles*** within the dockyard. ***Superb*** would later be taken into dry-dock for repairs and a short refit.

On Sunday 8 April colours were half-masted on the occasion of the funeral of the His Majesty King George of the Hellenes. The Royal ensign flew alongside the Greek ensign.

At 09.00 on 15 April 1947 Captain R M T Taylor DSC took command of ***Superb*** and the previous master Captain Robson left the ship at 13.30. The next day the dock was flooded as ***Superb*** was gently eased into No 1 Basin by harbour tugs before being moved to the West Wall. She remained there until Wednesday 30 April when she was moored alongside Farewell Jetty.

On 1 May 1947 ***Superb*** left Chatham and sailed to Portland where she would eventually spend most of May. During May 1947 *Superb* took part in the Cruiser Squadron Regatta. Winners from the competition were welcomed onboard ***Superb***, as flagship, where they were presented with prizes from Rear Admiral H A Parker CB.

On Friday 30 May ***Superb*** slipped from Portland and made the short passage to the Solent and Portsmouth with ***Sirius*** and the destroyer ***Myngs***. The force was 'attacked' by motor torpedo boats off the Hampshire coastline. At 14.33 *Superb* stopped engines in order to collect the local pilot who took the cruiser into Portsmouth harbour. As she was being eased onto her berth within the dockyard the tug ***Grapple*** damaged some of ***Superb's*** plates.

On Tuesday 2 June ***Superb*** returned to the Solent to carry out a series of practice shots at targets before sailing with the destroyer ***Aisne*** on a visit to Copenhagen in Denmark. A Mr Duffle from the BBC joined the cruiser for the passage, he recorded interviews with the officers and men of the ship for later broadcast. By Monday 9 June *Superb* had entered the Kattegat, whilst the following morning a pilot embarked to take the ship into Copenhagen harbour. At 08.17 she passed the impressive breakwater and fired a 21-gun salute before being secured alongside a jetty. Within hours the Mayor of the city paid a visit to the cruiser, as did Admiral Vedal, C-in-C of the Danish Navy. Both visitors were afforded full ceremonial honours. During the visit the ship was frequently open to the public. On one such occasion a woman visitor was taken ill and had to be rushed to hospital. Later the same day, His Excellency the British Ambassador, Admiral Anderson and Colonel Reese were welcomed onboard ***Superb*** and entertained by the Admiral until the small hours of Saturday morning.

Admiral Packer CB left the ship at 09.55 on Sunday 15 June to call on His Majesty King Frederick IV of Denmark. The following day having successfully completed a good visit the cruiser set sail at 09.02. Three hours later she passed eight Swedish minesweepers. Bad fog conditions slowed *Superb*'s progress the next morning as she made her way to Sweden, at times with just two cables visibility ahead.

By 17.12 ***Superb*** arrived at Stockholm and anchored in the outer harbour in 25 and a half fathoms of water. Two Swedish motor torpedo boats and a motor yacht were secured port side the following morning and Admiral Packer boarded one of the MTB's to take him ashore. At 11.45 with the fog finally clear ***Superb*** was allowed to proceed into Stockholm anchorage where she anchored at 16.10. The next morning the Swedish tug ***Strangaven*** came alongside the cruiser and secured a pontoon and gangway on the portside to allow visitors to easily board the cruiser. These visitors were at first high profile VIP's from the Swedish Navy, Government and the British Government.

The cruiser ***Dido*** joined ***Superb*** on Friday 20 June and were shackled together. A fire was discovered onboard ***Superb*** that afternoon in the Blacksmith's Shop, which was successfully extinguished by 14.30. The two Ships Company of officers arranged for the quarterdecks of both ships to be the site of an officer's dance. Awnings were put out over the quarterdeck and at 21.00 the dance began.

Another high profile visitor to the ***Superb*** was welcomed onboard on Saturday 21 June in the form of the Swedish Minister of Defence. He was followed in the afternoon by members of the public, who were genuinely fascinated by the British warships in their harbour.

The visit came to an end on Monday 23 June when ***Superb*** and ***Dido*** left Stockholm for Sheerness. The anchors were weighed at 17.15 and both ships headed to sea. ***Dido*** leading the destroyer ***Aisne*** and ***Superb*** at the rear. By Wednesday the three warships were joined by ***Cleopatra, Solebay*** and ***Gabbard***. Quickly the force was arranged with the three cruisers being screened by the destroyers. More warships joined on Thursday 26 with the addition of the aircraft carrier ***Vengeance*** and destroyers ***Sluys, Cadiz*** and ***Jutland***.

As they approached Sheerness the force was 'under attack' by aircraft from the Royal Air Force including Lancaster bombers, Hornets and the latest Meteor jets. At 18.30 on Friday 27 June ***Superb*** was alongside at Sheerness. She did not remain there long as the next day saw her crossing the Thames Estuary to anchor off the Essex seaside town of Southend for a five-day stay.

On Thursday 3 July the cruiser sailed north to Rosyth, where at 14.09 the following day she passed under the Forth Railway Bridge and passed ***Duke of York*** and the cruiser ***Diadem*** before anchoring at her berth twenty minutes later. On Sunday 6 July a flood was reported in No 2 store. Stoker's emergency parties were employed pumping out the compartment and found that 5lbs of leaf tobacco was destroyed by water damage.

Superb remained at anchor until the following Thursday when she picked up her anchor and sailed north with the rest of the fleet for Loch Ewe. During the passage 772 Squadron RAF made a series of dummy attacks on ***Sirius, Superb*** and ***Diadem*** with Mosquito fighter-bombers. ***Superb*** later broke off from the other two cruisers when a hospital case developed onboard and had to be taken to hospital at Aberdeen. The cruiser entered Aberdeen harbour at 13.38 and briefly anchored in 8 fathoms, but was soon back at sea once the seaman had been sent ashore.

At 16.25 a small fire was extinguished in the Shipwrights Shop before the ship arrived at Loch Ewe on Friday 11 July and anchored with the other cruisers who had been joined by ***Cleopatra***. On Tuesday 15 July all the cruisers in the squadron took part in the Squadron sailing race with whalers and dinghy's.

Two days later all the ships sailed for Gouroch and the Fleet Review planned for the Clyde. En route ***Superb*** exercised with the battleships ***Howe*** and ***Anson*** and the aircraft carriers ***Vengeance*** and ***Illustrious***. At the end of the day the ships anchored at Gouroch in preparation for the Royal Review on the Clyde. The next Sunday saw a rehearsal for the Royal visit and the ships were also open to the public.

Tuesday 22 July saw the arrival of the King and Queen to the Clyde and preparations for the visit took on an almost frantic affair onboard all the assembled ships in the Home Fleet. A Royal Guard was fallen in onboard ***Superb*** at 07.45 while other members of the ships company dressed the ship overall with flags and bunting. At 10.05 the order was given to fire a 21-gun salute to the Royal party as they boarded the cruiser for the first time during the Review. The Royals toured the ship until 19.55 when the Royal Party left the ship.

On Wednesday 23 July at 08.55 Divisions from ***Sirius, Dido, Diadem, Cleopatra*** arrived onboard ***Superb*** along with members of the press and masters of the assembled Royal Fleet Auxiliaries. An hour later, divisions for the Royal Inspection were fallen in. The Royal party sailed on a barge from Cardwell Bay to HMS ***Maidstone*** at 10.05 and after a brief tour of the depot ship eventually arrived at ***Superb*** at 10.45. The King and Queen were ceremonially piped onboard the flagship of the 2nd Cruiser Squadron. The King inspected the guard and was said to be very pleased with what he saw.

The Royal Party left ***Superb*** at 11.30 followed by representatives of the press. Mr A V Alexander, the Secretary of State of Scotland arrived onboard the cruiser and was ceremonially piped onboard. He had a private discussion with Admiral Packer before leaving the ship at 13.40 in the afternoon.

On Thursday 24 July ***Superb*** re-embarked the Royal Party for a trip around the Isle of Arran. The King and Queen arrived onboard at 10.45 and soon the ship was underway at 12 knots. The King and Queen left the ship at 12.10 but would return later in the day. They again left ***Superb*** at 18.56 for the final time that day.

On Sunday 27 July ***Superb*** and the rest of the fleet sailed for Cowes on the Isle of Wight. En route the force carried out a series of exercises with the battleship ***Duke of York***, the aircraft carrier ***Vengeance*** and the cruisers of the 2nd Cruiser Squadron. On the last day of July the convoy was attacked by RAF Meteors, Vampires and Beaufighters.

Superb arrived at Cowes at 08.17 on Thursday 31 July. She together with ***Illustrious***, ***Vengeance***, and the destroyer's ***Cadiz*** and ***Opportune*** detached from the main force and made for Spithead where ***Superb*** anchored at Cowes Roads at 11.14.

The Queen's birthday was celebrated on Monday 4 August when the ship was dressed overall. ***Superb*** remained at anchor until Sunday 10 August when she sailed to Portland. Three days were spent there before the cruiser sailed to Chatham, where she arrived at Thursday 14 August.

On Friday 19 September ***Superb*** returned to sea and made for Portland, where she arrived the next day. The cruiser remained at Portland until 2 October when she left to sea for-a days worth of exercises in the English Channel. This indeed turned out to be the pattern for the remainder of the month.

She slipped her moorings on Thursday 6 November and sailed to Spithead arriving just before eleven o'clock at night. Unable to enter Portsmouth Dockyard until the morning, she anchored in the Solent. By the morning ***Superb*** had entered Portsmouth Harbour and spent the weekend at No 6 buoy in Fountains Lake. 16.00 on Monday afternoon saw the cruiser once again slip and head to her anchorage in Spithead where she anchored overnight.

Tuesday 11 November ***Superb*** sailed to Weymouth Bay, where she would remain until 12 December except for one or two days at sea for exercises. On that day she sailed for Sheerness arriving later the same day. The cruiser's load of ammunition and stores were taken off the ship at Sheerness in a process that took the whole weekend to complete. On Monday 15 December she sailed the remainder of the way up the River Medway to Chatham Dockyard. She entered the North Lock at 12.30 and was soon within the safety of the dockyard. The following Thursday she was moved to No 9 dock by dockyard tugs for repairs and maintenance to be carried out on the ship.

On Friday 2 January 1948 the hands were employed restoring gear on the upper deck and painting between decks. The ship was moved from dry dock to No 3-basin NorthEast wall. By 10.05 she was secured to Farewell Jetty. The next morning an electrical fire broke out but was quickly brought under control.

The next Thursday ***Superb*** slipped from Chatham Dockyard and moved to Folly Point where ammunition and stores were loaded. She remained at Folly Point until Friday 23 January when she sailed for Portland. ***Superb*** arrived there the following morning and soon took her usual berth within the harbour.

On Thursday 5 February Superb took part in sea exercises off Portland that included dummy torpedo attacks before returning to Portland at 15.05 and secured to C4 buoy. ***Superb*** remained at her buoy until Tuesday 17 when together with the rest of the fleet sailed to Gibraltar. Later in the passage she carried out Night time encounter exercises with the 4th Destroyer Flotilla. Early in the morning of Wednesday ***Superb*** was the target for RAF aircraft from 19 Group. At 07.04 two Lancaster bombers carried out their attacks on the ship.

Saturday 21 February dawned bright and sunny as the ships arrived at Gibraltar. ***Superb*** was soon secured to Berth 46. The following Tuesday she was shifted from the South Mole to alongside at Flagstaff Jetty.

On 2 March a large force of American cruisers and destroyers left Gibraltar, these included USS ***Portsmouth, Gearing, Vogelsang, Eugene Greene*** and USS ***Grand Canyon.*** ***Superb*** sailed from Gibraltar to Portland on Thursday 11 March letting go her wires at 09.00. The passage back to the UK saw more exercises including an IFFX with the destroyer ***Agincourt.*** The British cruiser arrived back at Portland on Tuesday 16 March and saw the destroyers ***Battleaxe*** and ***Crossbow*** leave.

Three days later she sailed again back to Sheerness and onto Chatham. At Sheerness her load of ammunition was removed before completing the passage to Chatham on Tuesday 23 March at 10 knots.

Ship's Company *HMS Superb* 1954-55 *(W.D. Ross)*

Outside Bermuda at start of Commission *(E.G.R. Lee)*

Power trials off Bermuda, November 1954 *(W.D. Ross)*

Pom Pom Gun in action *(E.G.R. Lee)*

Jackstay Transfer to D25 *(E.G.R. Lee)*

From the aft deck of *HMS Implacable,* followed by the Battleships *Anson* and *Howe* in May 1954 *(AP)*

Weighing Anchor by Deck Tackle during Admirals Inspection *(W.D. Ross)*

A Torpedo comes inboard *(E.G.R. Lee)*

(E.G.R. Lee)

(Top & Bottom) Torpedo Firing During Admirals Inspection December 1954 *(W.D.Ross)*

Torpedoes Away! *(E.G.R. Lee)*

Ordnance and Shipwrights Department West Indies Station 1954-55 *(W.D. Ross)*

Entering Atlantic Side of the Panama Canal January 1955 *(W.D. Ross)*

Through Grenada's Palm Trees April 1955 *(W.D. Ross)*

Montego Bay, Jamaica During Spring Deployment 1955 *(W.D. Ross)*

An early photo of *Superb*, taken 1946, location unknown. *(MOD)*

Superb in 1955. This is a commemorative photo of the 1954-55 Commission. *(MOD)*

Superb remained at Chatham until Monday 26 April when she loaded her weapon load at Folly Point and continued her journey to Rosyth on Friday 30 April.

The first day of May 1948 saw ***Superb*** arrive at Rosyth. She was not alongside for long as on the following Monday 3 May she was at sea with ***Corunna, Agincourt, Jutland*** and ***Dunkirk*** bound for Largo Bay for exercises. Friday 7 May saw her return to Rosyth for leave to be granted. The following Wednesday ***Superb*** again sailed, this time for ***Exercise Dawn*** in the area around Scapa Flow. In the following weeks she paid visits to Nairn and Aberdeen. She sailed from Aberdeen on Monday 7 June bound for Rosyth.

More exercises took place North of Berwick from Wednesday 9 June that extended to an area around Kilkaldy Bay. ***Superb*** arrived back at Rosyth on Friday 11 June. The weekend saw the ship open to the public during Navy Week and many thousands of people toured the cruiser, with 1300 on the first day alone.

Tuesday 22 June ***Superb*** sailed to Anstruther for a two-day visit before returning to North Berwick where the ship was once again open to public inspection. The first day of July 1948 saw ***Superb*** weighing anchor at 21.00 and making the relatively short voyage to Scarborough. The cruiser anchored off the town on Friday 2 July and in short order welcomed onboard the Mayor of the town, followed by hundreds of local residents during the visit which ended on Friday 9 July. ***Superb*** sailed into the North Sea for exercises that culminated with her arrival back at Sheerness on Monday 12 July. At Sheerness she picked up No 1 buoy where ammunition was unloaded.

From Sheerness she sailed to Chatham on Thursday 15. She spent the whole at August at Chatham and was under refit for the whole of the remainder of 1948.

On 21 December 1948 Captain A K Scott-Moncrieff DSO took command. ***Superb*** remained at Chatham Dockyard until 26 January 1949 when she left the familiar dockyard surroundings to sail down the River Medway to Sheerness to take on ammunition. The following Sunday 30 January ***Superb*** left Sheerness and sailed down the British coastline to Spithead where she anchored overnight. The following day she entered 'D' lock at Portsmouth for another overnight stay. Having left Portsmouth Dockyard the cruiser anchored in St Helen's Roads anchorage for yet another overnight stay.

On Wednesday 2 February ***Superb*** sailed to Weymouth Bay and then onto Portland. Just two days were spent at Portland before she started her journey to Gibraltar on Saturday 5 February 1949. After four days steaming ***Superb*** arrived at Gibraltar along with a large force of Home Fleet units that included the battleship ***Vanguard*** and an escort of destroyers.

In the second week of March 1949, whilst operating out of Gibraltar, ***Theseus*** exercised with the battleship *Duke of York,* the fleet carrier ***Implacable*** and the cruiser ***Superb.***

On Monday 14 March ***Superb*** sailed for Casablanca, where she arrived the next day. As she approached her anchorage *Superb* fired a 13 gun salute for Rear Admiral Jozan of the French Navy, an eleven gun salute for Brigadier General Bureau and a nine gun salute for his Excellency Si Taier El Mouri, Pache de Casablanca. During her stay at Casablanca the ship was opened to visitors, whilst members of her crew ventured in land and the exotic nature of the culture at Casablanca.

The five-day visit was completed on Sunday 20 March when ***Superb*** sailed back to Sheerness, where after five days steaming north she arrived at Sheerness to unload her ammunition. The cruiser would spend five days at Buoy 2 in the River Medway before proceeding up river to Chatham Dockyard.

Chatham Navy Days allowed the people of the Medway Towns to explore 'their' cruiser over the Bank Holiday weekend. The remainder of April was spent alongside at Chatham with crew being granted seasonal leave with their families. ***Superb*** next ventured to sea on Tuesday 3 May when she left Chatham to load weapons at Folly Point off Sheerness. During this process the crew watched the unusual visitors to Sheerness in the form of two Swedish warships the ***Mangen*** and ***Tauri***. On 3 May 1949 Vice Admiral Sir Richard V Symonds Taylor, KBE, CB, DSC, Commander in Chief America and West Indies Station was appointed to his position onboard ***Superb***.

On Thursday 5 May 1949 ***Superb*** sailed north to Invergordon, where she arrived two days later. She would spend the remainder of the month in Scottish waters.

On 2 June the cruiser sailed to Scapa Flow and Cape Wraith before crossing the North Sea on Saturday 4 June to Copenhagen and a visit to the Danish Naval Base. She arrived on Monday morning and later in the day welcomed onboard the British Ambassador. During her stay at Copenhagen the cruiser was open to the public before sailing on Monday 13 June to Vinga Sound and the approaches to Gothenburg harbour at 16.30. She berthed in the harbour and watched as the Swedish cruiser *Gotland* arrived in port the next day. Again *Superb* was open for public scrutiny and the Swedish people proved to be very interested in the British cruiser on the Sunday of her visit, not fewer than 4,957 people toured the ship.

The next morning ***Superb*** sailed and headed south to Dover for a five-day visit from 22 June. En route she sighted the cruiser ***Cleopatra*** and ***Superb*** saluted the flag of CS 2 with 13-guns. ***Cleopatra*** returned the salute. ***Superb*** arrived at Dover and proved to be a major attraction for the cross channel port. Nearly 10,000 people visited the ship during her stay.

Monday 27 June saw ***Superb*** sail from Dover into poor visibility, which steadily improved as she made her way to Portland. Portland was reached the next day. Three days were spent at Portland, before ***Superb*** sailed to take part in Exercise Verity with French and Dutch warships off Penzance and in the English Channel. On Friday 8 July at the end of the exercises the Rear Admiral gave a press conference onboard whilst the ship was at anchor off Torquay. She remained at anchor for a few days and welcomed onboard a list of VIP's including local MP's and other dignitaries.

On Tuesday 12 July ***Superb*** left Torquay and headed along the coastline to Eastbourne and anchored in 9 and a half fathoms, where again she was opened to the public who were ferried out to the ship via small boats. ***Superb*** stayed at Eastbourne until Monday 18 July, when she made the relatively short voyage to Spithead.

Two days were spent at anchor in the Solent before she raised steam and sailed back to Sheerness, where she arrived later the same day. At Sheerness the usual process of offloading her ammunition and stores took until the following Monday. On that day ***Superb*** sailed to Chatham and at 13.57 entered No 3 Basin within the dockyard.

The following Saturday, Sunday and Bank Holiday Monday saw the dockyard thrown open to the general public for Navy Days.

Monday 5 September saw *Superb* return to sea when she arrived at Sheerness to load ammunition, fuel and stores. Once completed the cruiser continued onto Sandown Bay on the Isle of Wight and from there, operated with the aircraft carrier *Vengeance* and the destroyer *Finnisterre*. On Sunday 11 September she sailed from Cowes to Shoeburyness in Essex. At Shoeburyness she anchored in 10 fathoms and the ammunition lighter, *Duckling*, came alongside and filled up the cruisers supply of ammunition. Superb fired some rounds at the Army firing range during her stay off Essex, which came to an end on Friday 16 September. *Superb* continued to chart a course, northwards to Rosyth and at 15.48 she was passing under the Forth Bridge.

The weekend was spent alongside, with many of the crew having been granted leave to enjoy in Edinburgh. On Monday 19 September it was back to sea for ***Superb*** as she together with the rest of the Home Fleet made for Invergordon for exercises that also saw the cruiser operate in Cromarty Firth and Spey Bay. On Monday 3 October she arrived at Loch Eriboll for more exercises. Exercise Skaal took place from Wednesday 12 October and took ***Superb*** to Methil along with the destroyer ***Battleaxe***. At Methil she was open to the public before leaving on the following Thursday. She made for Rosyth where she arrived later on the same day.

At Rosyth ***Superb*** took on 492 tons of furnace oil from RFA ***Black Ranger***. On 25 October the cruiser left Rosyth and headed for Glasgow via the North of Scotland. ***Superb*** nosed her way through the shipping in the Clyde before arriving at Glasgow's Springfield Quay at 16.12 on Thursday 27 October. For the next week dignitaries, local celebrities and the general public streamed over the cruiser, whilst members of the crew enjoyed well-earned leave in the city.

The visit came to an end on the 4th November when Superb sailed to Lamlash, where she spent the weekend at anchor. Monday morning steam was raised and ***Superb*** sailed south to Portland with the aircraft carrier ***Implacable*** the cruiser ***Diadem*** and the 5th Destroyer Flotilla. ***Superb*** was in a position behind the destroyer ***Wizard***. At Portland the ships took part in Exercise *Porcupine* and Exercise Winkle. By Saturday 12 November ***Superb*** was at anchor at Portland where she stayed until the following Tuesday for the second phase of Exercise ***Winkle***.

On Monday 21 November ***Superb*** sailed back to Folly Point in Kent and started the process of unloading her ammunition into lighters from Sheerness Dockyard. Once completed on Friday 25 the cruiser sailed to Chatham Dockyard and secured in No 2 Basin in preparation for a lengthy refit. In December she was taken into No 9 Dock for a refit which started on 6 December.

On 1 January 1950 ***Superb*** was in No 9 dock at Chatham where she remained for another three days until on Wednesday 4 January she was moved to the South side of No 3 Basin. The day also saw the change of command ceremony when Superb's latest commanding officer, Captain Sir Anthony W Buzzard DSO OBE took command. On Tuesday 17 January ***Superb*** was towed by tugs to Folly Point off Sheerness and was loaded with weaponry

Monday 23 January dawned cold but the cruiser sailed from Folly Point to Portland later that day around 13.40. As she left the River Medway the tugs ***Adherence*** and ***Egerton*** were on hand to assist. By 14.46 she had passed Garrison Point at 12 knots and formed up with the cruiser ***Cleopatra*** and destroyers ***Solebay, Gabbard*** and ***Crossbow***.

The following day at 08.02 in the English Channel ***Superb*** test fired the 6-inch guns in 'A' turret, before securing to B1 buoy at Portland just after four in the afternoon. ***Superb*** remained at the buoy until Saturday 28 when she sailed for Gibraltar at the start of Exercise ***Golden Fish***.

On Sunday 29th January 1950 ***Superb*** was at sea with the battleship ***Vanguard***, the carriers ***Victorious, Implacable*** and destroyers including ***Alamein, Cadiz, Gabbard*** and ***St James***. ***Vengeance*** joined the force this day as they sailed to Gibraltar and the Mediterranean. On 2 February the ships arrived at Gibraltar where they stayed except for exercises until 16 February when ***Superb*** sailed in company with the destroyer ***Crossbow*** on a visit to Madeira. The crews of both ships were granted shore leave for the four-day visit.

The rest of February was spent in and around Gibraltar except for the time between 18 and 22nd February when ***Superb*** along with the destroyer ***Battleaxe*** paid a visit to Madeira. Having returned to Gibraltar on February 24 the Royal Navy force sailed for Palmas Bay in early March. On 8 March ***Superb*** arrived at Rapallo with the destroyer ***Corunna*** and later also visited Cagliari.

A combined fleet gathering at Gibraltar started on 22 March, which saw ***Vengeance, Implacable*** and ***Superb*** sail from Gibraltar for Exercise ***Artful Antic*** a week later. At the end of the exercise all the ships returned to their homeports with ***Superb*** arriving at Sheerness on 3 April before proceeding to Chatham some time later.

Superb was back at sea on 13 May and spent a week at Portland until 21 May when she sailed south to Quiberon Bay and Dourarnerez Bay as part of a two-day Western Union Exercise ***Activity***. The exercise was designed to test and improve communications, plotting and anti submarine and anti-aircraft skills. The British ships taking part included the aircraft carrier ***Implacable, Cleopatra, Agincourt, Jutland, Battleaxe, Crossbow*** and the submarines ***Aurochs*** and ***Trespasser***. These ships were joined by French ships, ***George Leygues, Le Fantasque*** and the ***Karel Dorman, Jacob Van Heemskerck, Johan Maurits van Nassau, Marnix*** and the submarines ***Zwaardvis, Dolfijn*** and ***0.27***. ***Superb's*** crew enjoyed runs ashore and one of the most popular destinations was Brest, which was visited from 27 May. For some three days was insufficient but the cruiser sailed back to Portland. On 2 June she crossed the English Channel once more to visit St Peters Port in the Channel Islands and then steamed northwards through the Pas de Calais and on into the North Sea.

Superb had been invited to visit Sweden and the opportunity was hard to resist. The cruiser sailed through the Kattegate and into the Baltic Sea before arriving at the scenic port of Goteburg on 7 June. The welcome afforded the crew was truly stunning and many found it hard to leave on 12 June. After two days steaming in the Baltic, the Swedish Capital City of Stockholm was visited. Many VIP's and celebrities toured the ship during her weeklong stay. On 21 June ***Superb*** started the journey back to Invergordon during which, she undertook a fleet exercise. July 1950 also saw the cruiser pay visits to Dundee, South Shields and on 22 July she anchored off the pier at Southend for four days. Finally on 26 July ***Superb*** arrived at Sheerness, where her ammunition was unloaded.

The summer months of 1950 were spent at Chatham under repair and to allow the crew-leave. Chatham Navy Days of this year saw ***Superb*** open to the public but by the beginning of autumn the ship was ready again for sea and the crew had returned to the cruiser. ***Superb*** would in late 1950 become closely associated with the West Indies when she was ordered to relieve the cruiser ***Glasgow***. On 1 November under the command of Captain W J Yendell ***Superb*** left Chatham bound for Portsmouth, where she arrived three days later. A further brief stop at Portland was followed by an eight day stay at Gibraltar for work up's. On 21 November ***Superb*** started the crossing to Bermuda where she arrived nine days later.

Superb was flagship of the American and West Indies Squadron flying the flag of Vice Admiral Sir Richard Symonds Taylor. Bermuda was considered one of the jewels in the Caribbean with blue skies, warm sea and pink beaches but with very expensive runs ashore. This was more than compensated by local cheap Rum and Coke at HMS *Malabar* and swimming in the sea on Christmas Day. ***Superb*** slipped back to sea on 5 January when she headed towards Cuba.

Guantanamo Bay was reached on 8 January. ***Superb*** arrived at the American Naval Base and saw that HMS ***Sparrow*** and HMS ***Bigbury Bay*** were also present. The three ships soon exercised with the American Fleet, which included 4" AA shoots on aircraft towed targets as well as 6" full calibre shoots. Sailors recalled that there were 'big eats' and cheap drinks at the American PX.

Superb sailed to Trinidad on 13 January for a brief two-day stopover. En route to Rio the cruiser 'crossed the line' and King Neptune and his court made a spectacular appearance and 'punishments' were handed out to offenders. Before *Superb*'s arrival at Rio the crew painted the ship with all hands in cradles over the sides. The painters worked quickly due to the threat of sharks, but the Chief Gunners Mate was on deck with a rifle. Finally, looking splendid, ***Superb*** pulled into Rio de Janeiro on 29 January. The cruiser going alongside the Brazilian Naval Dockyard. Several other ships followed her in including ***Bigbury Bay***, the US heavy cruiser ***Albany***, a Chilean transport and two Peruvian frigates. The occasion was the inauguration of the newly elected President Vargas. The 3rd February was the first day of the Mardi Gras. There was much partying and decorated floats and sailors recalled seeing almost everybody having an aerosol and squirting everybody else; it seemed intoxicating, the cans were believed to contain ether.

Whilst at Rio sailors from the cruiser took the opportunity to climb up the base of the Cocavada, that well known statue of Christ or to Copacabana beach. It wasn't all play; however, in Rio where it was carnival time for four days and nights the British Guard Band and seamen were on parade at attention for nearly 3 hours in temperatures of 113 degrees. It so stirred the inhabitants that the Marines and sailors were virtually mobbed on returning to the ship. The same thing happened later during a visit to Montevideo.

On 12 February 1951 the cruiser sailed into the bleak harbour at Port Stanley. The Falkland Islands welcomed the ship with cold and wet weather conditions. ***Superb*** anchored in the outer harbour. The sailors all recall the bleakness of the environment around the island's capital, Port Stanley, where there were no trees and most of the buildings were constructed out of corrugated iron.

On February 16 ***Superb*** sailed north through an iceberg field, which had more than 150 'bergs and the field covered around 70 miles.

After four days steaming North, ***Superb*** arrived at Buenos Aires and entered port with the ship's company fallen in on the Upper Deck in No.6's (best whites) for a visit by President and Eva Peron at 11am on 22 February. The ship had organised a huge bouquet of flowers for Mrs Peron. However 20 minutes after they were due to arrive a message was received saying that they would not be coming. The Peron's had deliberately snubbed the cruiser after Eva Peron had been refused an audience with the Queen when she was in London. Serious diplomatic activity ensued with resulted in an apology being received and arrangements for the Admiral to be received by President Peron that evening. With the frosty reception behind them, *Superb*'s cruise in South American waters continued with an official visit on 27 February to the Capital City of Uruguay, Montevideo.

The two cities were only a relatively short distance apart across the Rio de la Plata, but the reception was the polar opposite from that in Buenos Aires. In Montevideo the ship was welcomed like friends.

A further five days were spent at the holiday resort of, Punta del Este before sailing on 12 March 1951 for Puntas Arenas in Argentina. At Punta Arenas there was a banyan arranged to a meatpacking Plant. Literally sheep were driven in one end and there were carcasses ready for the freezer. The crew was invited to a meal, which consisted of great trays of lamb with very little vegetables or potatoes. Around the bay for hundreds of yards alongside the packing plant the sea was stained red with blood and waste from the plant.

From Puntas Arenas ***Superb*** sailed to her next destination of Valparaiso in Chile on 26 March. Sailors from the ***Superb*** reminisced about possibly the best run ashore of the whole cruise. A tenner bought all the wine that sailors could possibly need and also huge plates of food and anything else they might require too. On a more sombre note the residents of Valparaiso took the opportunity offered by *Superb*'s visit to inaugurate a new tomb and memorial for British sailors buried in the city. The Captain and Guard and Band took part in the ceremony.

At Callao, the port of Lima, ***Superb*** spent five glorious days from 5 April. There were a number of events arranged for members of the Ship's Company, one of which was a trip to the Trans-Andean Railway. This railway is the highest standard gauge railway in the world rising to 15,000feet. The trip was not organised to go that high but to a mining village, Rio Blanca at 12,500feet and expected to take 12 hours. From Chile, ***Superb*** continued northwards and exercised with local forces in the region before arriving on 14 April at Balboa and the entrance to the Panama Canal. ***Superb*** passed through the three locks at each end of the canal and in the centre Gatum Lake. Having successfully navigated the waterway and entered the Caribbean ***Superb*** made port at Bermuda on 20 April. Soon after her arrival a change of command took place and ***Superb*** was transferred to the command of Captain E W J Bankes. Bermuda also saw an incident when ***Superb***'s oil barge was sunk.

The barge was 60 feet long and held 300 tons of fuel. During the process of filling the barge improper loading caused it to list so badly it flooded and sank. The barge promptly started to release oil into the harbour and a boom was erected across Clarence Cove to protect the precious marine environment.

With the boom in place came the hard and dangerous task of raising the barge from the bottom. *Superb*'s three divers with the limited equipment onboard spent many hours underwater sealing all vents and hatches in order to blow air into the barge in order to re-float it. With air being pumped in, the fuel and water mixture was pumped out through a special adapter made on *Superb*. The process continued for many hours until suddenly and without any warning the barge shot to the surface and came within a hair's breath of sinking the diving boat. One diver, Bernie Robertson, who was underwater at the time, was lucky to escape with his life.

Back onboard *Superb* when the divers stripped off their equipment, it had been ruined, by the thick oil and much of it needed to be replaced or extensively cleaned. The oil also caused the unfortunate death of the Diving Stores parakeet after being soaked in oil. All three divers received commendations for their work.

After this drama, Guantanamo Bay came as a pleasant relief when from 18 June *Superb* exercised with the American fleet stationed on Cuba. She remained off the island until 29 June. An overnight passage placed the cruiser at Kingstown, Jamaica the following morning. The cruiser visited numerous British dependencies in the Caribbean throughout the next week including the Virgin Islands and Culebra. She also paid a brief visit to Puerto Rico. By 9 July she was back at Bermuda where she stayed until 23 July undertaking a period of alongside maintenance.

Superb continued Northwards and along the coastline of America's Southern States until she reached Norfolk Naval Station on 25 July. On arrival *Superb* was under strict instructions that under no circumstances was she to fire her 6-inch guns whilst lying alongside the wall. Later during the two-day visit, Vice Admiral Symonds Taylor called on Admiral Fechterler, the American Admiral, then C-in-C Atlantic Fleet.

Superb slipped into the North Atlantic on 27 July and again set a course northwards for her next destination of St Johns in Newfoundland where she arrived on the last day of July. At St John's many of the locals had Irish accents. Being a seafaring community, the local women vastly outnumbered men, the men folk having suffered a high loss of life during World War Two. This made for a very interesting six-day stopover for many amongst the crew.

The Canadian leg of the cruise continued with a visit to the Royal Canadian Navy Base at Halifax from 8 August. *Superb*'s crew participated in a parade and Naval March Past held to welcome the cruiser to the city. During the visit Sir Richard Symonds Taylor presented the Canadians with the ships bell from the old frigate HMS *Shannon*. The bell had hung in Bermuda for over 100 years and the opportunity was taken to present it on the occasion of the establishment of a new naval facility named HMS Shannon. Local children at Halifax were entertained with a circus afloat. The crew dressed up in animal costumes and made pirates 'walk the plank' into icy waters and thrilling rides for the youngsters in the bosuns chair.

Canada has two towns called St Johns and ***Superb*** visited the second from 16 August. The men from the cruiser, unfortunately, found life at St Johns a little tame with no nightlife but nice welcoming people. During the four-days spent at the New Brunswick town the crew donated a total of fifty-two bottles of blood for troops wounded in Korea.

Superb returned to sea on 20 August and headed south to Bar Harbour in Maine. The journey took only a few hours and when the cruiser arrived she anchored half a mile offshore before going alongside later in the day. The crew enjoyed seven days of local attractions that included the world renowned Jones Beach State Park with some of Long Islands best beaches. Boating and nautical activities were also laid on.

An overnight passage on 27 August positioned ***Superb*** at the entrance to Newport, Rhode Island the next morning. The locals at the city laid on excellent hospitality and entertainment. At Newport the crew played the Americans at softball and at cricket. The Americans predictably won the softball while the British won the game of Cricket.

From Newport another overnight journey began on 4 September which brought ***Superb*** to the wide expanse of the historic Boston Harbour, famous for the Boston Tea Party. The locals were proud of their heritage but still welcomed the British cruiser with great enthusiasm. One of the reasons for the visit was to coincide with British Trade Fortnight, which was opened by the Admiral. The Americans lent Superb eight television sets to view local American TV. The verdict from *Superb*'s crew was that it was 'It was commercial and it was awful!"

Whilst in Boston several of the ship's company were paid $5 for a pint of blood, with the money allowing the men to enjoy themselves on runs ashore. One sailor trying to make more money donated three pints and promptly collapsed. Nursed back to health and diagnosed with acute anaemia he was given a blood transfusion and charged $25!

Philadelphia was next on the itinerary but whilst the city was very interesting, there was a sometimes over powering smell in the air from the heavy industry that dominated the city. Crewmembers recall it being like London's smog.

Superb sailed for what was undoubtedly the highlight of the cruise, the city of New York on 20 September. The overnight passage was uneventful as the cruiser arrived off the Hudson River the next day. ***Superb*** arrived off Brooklyn and the Statue of Liberty and anchored for a few hours waiting for the ***Queen Mary*** to clear her berth. The cruiser then was given the honour of being escorted into port with New York's fireboats flamboyant water display on show. The British cruiser berthed at Pier 90. The liner ***Mauritania*** arrived on 24 September and berthed on the opposite side. During the stay ***Queen of Bermuda*** and ***Queen Monarch*** also docked nearby. The size of the ***Queen Elizabeth*** meant that ***Superb*** was moved to Pier 26 to allow the passenger liner to dock at the Cunard Pier, Pier 90. A large number of trips had been laid on for the crew including sightseeing tours of Radio City and the Empire State Building.

After her visit to New York ***Superb*** sailed back to Bermuda where she arrived on 1 October. The next eighteen days were spent at the island. News of the loss of the submarine ***Affray*** and the loss of lives saw *Superb*'s complement work to raise money for their dependants. The cruiser's amateur dramatic company put on a show in Bermuda and made history by filling the new theatre called The Bermudiana for the first time in its history. Over £400 was raised at two performances of the show and one very generous audience member donated £100 for his seat.

The cruiser was joined in harbour by ***Sheffield***, who after a week with ***Superb*** assumed flagship duties allowing the latter to start for home on 19 October.

At 07.00 on 29 October ***Superb*** secured with double bridles to No 2 buoy at Sheerness to de-ammunition and watched as the Danish frigate ***Neils Ebberson*** left harbour. By 11.30 the, ammunition had been offloaded and the cruiser proceeded up the River Medway but only as far as Folly Point where she secured. On Wednesday 31 October ***Superb*** entered Chatham Dockyard and was later in November moved to No 9 dock for repairs to be undertaken.

On 16 November the, dry-dock was flooded and ***Superb*** was towed out to be berthed alongside the North Wall of No 3 Basin. At 11.40 there was a small fire onboard in the vicinity of No 7 Power Room, but it was quickly extinguished. The following Saturday 28 students from Wye College arrived onboard to be given a guided tour of the cruiser. The remainder of December 1951 was spent in Basin 3 at Chatham Dockyard.

At the beginning of January 1952 in the re-organisation of the Home Fleet *Superb* was designated Flag Ship for the Flag Officer Flotilla's, Home Fleet. The cruiser headed to sea on 12 January and set a course for Nassau for a four-day stay at the island. With the sound of steel bands still ringing in their ears the crew of *Superb*'s next destination would give them another chance to experience the Caribbean beat at Trinidad. Just three days were spent there before proceeding onto the Falkland Islands. At Port Stanley Superb delivered post and medical officers checked over the various ailments of the local residents during a three-day stay. All too soon Superb was back at sea and headed northwards along the South American coastline and made calls at Montevideo and Buenos Aires. At the Argentinean city the reception was substantially less frosty than on the previous occasion.

From Buenos Aires, *Superb* visited the city of Rio de Janeiro and experienced life on the beach and in the city's bars and restaurants. On 16 March 1952 *Superb* left Rio and returned to the Caribbean Sea. The last few days of the month saw the cruiser visiting Trinidad, and Barbados before arriving back at Bermuda.

On Tuesday 1 April 1952 *Superb* was at Chatham awaiting the large crowds that would no doubt visit the ship during the upcoming Chatham Navy Days. Saturday 12 April was the first of three days set aside for the annual event and no fewer that 3990 people chose to look around *Superb*. Sunday's figure was even better at 5549 visitors and Monday's topped even that impressive figure at a, staggering 7150 visitors.

The Queen's birthday on 21 April saw the ship dressed overall with flags. Superb remained at Chatham until being towed out to Folly Point on Monday 12 May. Three days later she returned to Chatham Dockyard and secured alongside Basin 3 in the dockyard and by Monday 19 May 1952 her refit was started in earnest. On Saturday 24 May in a ceremony staged at 08.00 the Flag of FOFH was transferred from *Superb* to her half sister *Swiftsure* and Admiral W G A Robson left the ship to join the *Swiftsure* along with his staff officers. *Superb*'s refit at Chatham would not be completed until 29 August 1952.

In early September 1952 *Superb* slipped out of Chatham Dockyard with large patches of red lead and a thick coating of dockyard grime. It was a cold, grey and wet day at Sheerness when shells and provisions were loaded onboard and the final coats of paint were applied to the cruiser's sides and upper-works. The intention had been to steam to Portland but leaky steam joints put pay to this and *Superb* returned to Chatham on 16 September. On entering the South Lock Superb rammed herself into the dock and wouldn't budge for the next 24 hours. Eventually she was freed and entered Chatham Dockyard for a number of repairs to be undertaken.

When *Superb* left she sailed North to Rosyth arriving at the Scottish naval base on 12 October. More repairs were undertaken at Rosyth but the efforts of the dockyard workers proved successful. When she sailed to join the Home Fleet at Invergordon for the fleet regatta her crew had high hopes. *Superb's* teams, however, proved no match for the rest of the fleet returning without any trophies.

Superb returned to Rosyth on 29 October and started her preparations for a cruise in the Caribbean that started on another cold grey November day as the warship passed under the red painted steel of the Forth Bridge.

Superb steered a course through a peaceful Pentland Firth and onto Bermuda some 3000 miles across the North Atlantic. On arrival at Grassy Bay *Superb* was surprised to find heavy seas, strong winds and a torrential downpour - unusual weather for

Bermuda. Christmas Day was spent alongside and *Superb* eventually put to sea again on 12 January 1953.

The passage to Nassau was a smooth one with many sailors beginning to sport a healthy looking suntan, although as usual some crewmembers over did the sunbathing and took on an unsightly lobster pink complexion. Nassau was reached on 15 January. After many hours spent on beautiful beaches and strolling through exclusive resorts, *Superb's* men had spent most of their money, but always managed to save some for the town's nightlife. Four days later Superb sailed for Trinidad. The trip took an unexpected turn when en-route large sheets of paint started to peel from the ships' sides. Immediate painting sessions cured the situation in time for the cruiser's arrival in Port of Spain.

Before arriving at Port of Spain the crew busied themselves in painting the ships' sides despite the threat posed by sharks and barracudas. Even with the sharks some crewmembers decided it was worth the risk for a refreshing swim. Once painted *Superb* looked splendid as she passed through 'The Dragon's Mouth at 08.30 on 23 January 1953. Trinidad was, and still is a luxuriously forested volcanic island. *Superb* went alongside at the King's Wharf, where it was very hot. Local attractions soon became big draws for the crew including the famous Maracas Beach. *Superb* had arrived during calypso week and as a result there was much partying made better by visits to Ancostura Bitters. Steel drum bands played onboard the cruiser one evening and were very popular. *Superb* sailed on 26 January with an over abundance of local fruit filling the ship to the gunnels.

Five days later bound for Bahia amongst much ceremonial and conch-shell blowing, King Neptune and his court arrived on board. The day was given over to the initiation of the many quaking novices.

Superb arrived at Bahia, the port of Salvador in Brazil on the 4th February. One of the highlights of the visit was when the Royal Marines elected to Beat Retreat twice in the evening at the local stadium. A crowd of some 1,500 saw the first performance whilst the second attracted a crowd of about 5000.

After a two-day visit, the ship sailed for the Falkland Islands. Progressively the weather turned colder and the sea took on a much darker colour. After five-days in rising seas *Superb* made port at Port Stanley and anchored out of sight of the town at the start of a six-week long stay at the Falklands.

The Royal Marines onboard *Superb* left the cruiser for the six-weeks to carry out policing duties across the islands. The 600 plus crewmembers almost doubled the population of Port Stanley, but the inhabitants coped well with the extra people. During the stay crewmembers went ashore and took part in shooting parties for hare and goose, although the results were disappointing. What was not, however, in short supply was mutton, or locally known as 'Falkland Islands Venison'

When the cruiser left the Falklands on 25 March she sailed into a band of fine weather that quickly slipped away and was replaced by a spell of strong winds as Superb headed northwards. *Superb's* next destination was Rio de Janeiro, where she arrived in the early morning of 31 March. The familiar sights of Sugar Loaf mountain, the Corcovado and Copacabana beach came into view soon enough as Superb eased into Rio harbour with its modern skyscrapers.

Only two days were spent in Rio, but those 48 hours were a host of experiences for the crew, many of who found bars in the city, others climbed mountains and others sunned themselves on the clean, wide beaches. The ship sailed for Trinidad on 11 April arriving five days later. When she anchored the opportunity was taken to renew the cruiser's paintwork, such was the need for the paint job that it took four days to complete the work.

News was received soon thereafter that *Superb* would be part of the fleet being assembled for the Coronation Review. Four days after leaving Trinidad *Superb* arrived at Bermuda on the 20 April, where the Bermuda Corporation contingent and some 50 odd passengers were embarked, and sailed for Chatham on the 30th April.

The North Atlantic was quiet and the crossing uneventful and *Superb* re-entered the River Medway on 10 May. Ten days leave was granted to each watch. Upon their return some hard-days work preparing the ship and crew for the Review lay ahead. *Superb* left Sheerness on 5 June for Portland and eventually sailed for Spithead on the 9 June and berthed alongside the cruiser's *Sheffield* and *Swiftsure*. Superb represented the America and West Indies Squadron.

Having spent the best part of two months in Home waters *Superb* sailed to resume her West Indies duties and arrived back at Bermuda on 26 June. The North American cruise began with a visit to Boston on Thursday 16 July at 08.15. On entering Boston Harbour a National Salute was fired by Superb. Promptly at 09.00 the ship went alongside at the army base at Boston after being played in by a US Navy band.

In Boston the Royal Marines onboard *Superb* made history when they became the first British men under arms to parade on Boston Common with bayonets fixed and the first to discharge firearms since the American War of Independence. On both Saturday and Sunday of the visit *Superb* was opened to the public and 3263 people toured the ship. Young American boys equipped with screwdrivers were discovered busy removing items of the ship as souvenirs. The items were returned to their rightful place and the boys kindly asked to leave the ship. Other better-behaved children were invited to a children's party on Thursday 21st.

At 17.30 on 24 July 1953 *Superb* wearing the broad pennant of Commodore R. Tosswill OBE sailed from Boston for Portland, Maine famous for great scenery and equally delicious lobster. In 1953 Portland was not a big town, with a population of around 80,000. Despite this the locals welcomed the British warship and crew with open arms and took many to restaurants where New England lobster meals were served.

On 3 August *Superb* anchored a mile offshore of the summer resort town of Bar Harbour on Mount Desert Island. From Bar Harbor the ship sailed to Halifax in Nova Scotia. At 07.30 on Saturday 8 August *Superb* berthed at Wharf Number 5 in HMCS Dockyard Halifax, immediately below HMCS *Stadacona*, the RCN shore depot. Superb represented the Royal Navy at Canada's Navy Day and large numbers of ships, plus US Navy's 2nd Carrier Division headed up by the aircraft carrier USS *Bennington* were present. The Navy Day programme included a parade through the streets of Halifax in the morning followed by the opening of the Dockyard and individual ships to the public, of which 4,229 toured *Superb*.

The Royal Canadian Navy did all they could to make *Superb's* stay pleasant. The planned departure from Halifax did not go according to plan due to a Hurricane that swept through the region. When *Superb* did, eventually, leave port it was at 09.00 on Sunday 16 August.

After Halifax came St John's in Newfoundland. The cruiser entered the Narrows as she approached her destination. The Narrows were bordered on both sides by a ring of steep hills. The cruiser passed the site high on the cliff where the tower from which Marconi sent his first trans-Atlantic signals is sited. *Superb's* crew witnessed the town's rowing regatta and enjoyed a variety of good entertainment and good food during the visit.

Having left St John's *Superb* sailed onto the joint United States Navy and United States Air Force base at Argentia. Situated at the head of Placentia Bay the base was where the Atlantic Charter was signed. *Superb* arrived on the 21 August for a four-day visit. The Americans allowed the British men to use all the bases' facilities. The cruiser sailed up the Saint Lawrence in darkness, arriving at Quebec on the morning of the 27th August.

The ship berthed in Wolfe's Cove under the Heights of Abraham, nearby the Plains of Abraham was the scene of the famous battle between Wolfe and Montcalm. Quebec is dominated by the Chateau Frontenac an enormous and elite hotel. During the cruiser's stay at Quebec the crew made many visits ashore and enjoyed many of the local sports - albeit without much success most of the fishing and shooting being out of season. Many former crewmembers recall the magnificent daytime passage on the St Lawrence River to Gaspe. The journey was made unforgettable by the scenic splendour and the unique Gaelic style of churches in the occasional villages along the banks of the river.

Superb arrived at Gaspe on the 5th September. Gaspe is famous for its outstanding fishing and shooting - but of more note to the crew of *Superb* was the news of the murder of four tourists in recent months. Fortunately nothing untoward occurred during the visit. Gaspe was also the site of a large scale copper mining industry but this caused no ill effect on the population of cod in the harbour and many a fish supper was served onboard *Superb*.

Gaspe was a small Canadian town, but throughout the four-day stay the Mayor and citizens bent over backwards to entertain the British visitors. Some might say too well, as it was discovered the locals were partial to a good drink or three.

After Gaspe *Superb* arrived at Newport, Virginia on the penultimate port visit of the North American tour. The crew saw huge homes with gloriously well-manicured lawns and gardens in an area favoured by America's rich and elite. The stay in Newport was very enjoyable and made more so by the 500 lovely ladies who visited the ship and a seemingly never -ending river of beer. The last port to be visited on the tour was New York where *Superb* arrived on 22 September and berthed alongside Pier 92.

New York was exhilarating for the crew, especially those, who had never seen Manhattans skyscrapers before. New York was a hectic and frantic city full of attractions including the Empire State Building, Times Square, Chinatown and Broadway. Some crewmembers found time to walk down Broadway at night to see a star or two.

Superb sailed from New York at 28 knots on 20 September and sped for Bermuda. The reason for the speed became apparent when news reached the lower decks that communist inspired troubles were threatened at Georgetown in British Guiana. After fuelling at Bermuda, Superb made for Kingston, Jamaica and embarked the whole of the First Battalion of the Welsh Fusiliers.

On 4 October, after only hours alongside *Superb* slipped to sea once more bound for Trinidad. When she reached the Gulf of Paria, *Superb* anchored at night and over the next few hours transferred half of the soldiers to the frigates *Bigbury Bay* and *Burghead* Bay. *Superb* continued onto Georgetown in British Guiana, where Communist troubles were brewing. The remainder of the Welsh fusiliers; were landed on the 8 October in difficult conditions. The Royal Marines landed with the Army and *Superb* remained off Georgetown for the next three days until the situation calmed. After retrieving the Marines, *Superb* sailed for Trinidad and stayed there until relieved as flagship by *Sheffield* on 21 October. *Superb's* next duty was to return home and accordingly she made for Bermuda at the start of a Trans-Atlantic crossing.

At Bermuda Vice Admiral Andrewes bade farewell to the cruiser. The crossing was an unpleasant one with heavy seas all the way to Chatham Dockyard. Upon her return to the Kent dockyard she was taken in hand for a much-needed refit.

Superb remained in refit at Chatham until 22nd January 1954 and eventually ventured to sea on 3 February to join other members of the Home Fleet on a Mediterranean Cruise. *Superb* joined the battleship *Vanguard, Eagle, Apollo, Diamond, Duchess,* and *Decoy* to make their way to Gibraltar, which was reached on 8 February. Superb remained in and around the British colony for most of February only leaving on 26 February for a visit to Tangiers. The four-day visit was a success with many local dignitaries boarding the cruiser for guided tours. *Superb* sailed on 2 March and returned to Gibraltar. Mid March 1954 saw the cruiser take part in a four-day long exercise called CFX-'A' off Gibraltar. Finally on 28 March *Superb* sailed for Sheerness, where she arrived on 2 April.

Superb was due for refit at Chatham on 12 April 1954 that continued until 19 August 1954. During her refit 4000 square feet of ***Superb's*** quarterdeck was caulked with Secomastic compound using a Secomastic gun. This operation took place in varying weather conditions. On 23 and 24 August 1954 the ship was at sea doing a speed trial in rough wet weather and it was noticed that under these conditions the compound was creeping up and out of the seams. As a result nearly all was removed leaving only 250 feet over the Captain's cabin.

Superb commissioned at Chatham on 27 August 1954 and joined the Fleet Flotilla's and would in October deploy to the West Indies. ***Superb*** left Chatham on 1 October and made for Portland from where she crossed the North Atlantic bound for Bermuda. She made landfall on 18 October.

October and November also saw ***Superb*** spend time with the US Navy at Guantanamo Bay in Cuba. With the exercises completed the British cruiser arrived at Bermuda on 30 November.

On Wednesday 1 December 1954 ***Superb*** was alongside at Bermuda and the next day saw the arrival of the Canadian frigate HMCS ***Penetang,*** later in the day the submarine HMS ***Alcide*** secured alongside the cruiser at 17.20 in the afternoon. ***Alcide*** remained alongside for the next four days when she slipped to continue independent operations. An oil fire broke out ashore in the dockyard at 15.30 the next day. Fire fighters from the cruiser were dispatched to assist those from the dockyard and the fire was brought swiftly under control. Later in the same day ***Superb*** moved to Grassy Bay in Hamilton and on the 9 December the Royal Marine Band was landed to play at Admiralty House.

On Saturday 11 December ***Superb*** was opened to the public and by the time the ship was closed to visitors, 527 had passed through the cruiser. Sunday dawned with instructions that the British warship should return to the dockyard at Bermuda and by the next day she was secured alongside.

Saturday 1 January 1955 saw the cruiser alongside at Bermuda and she remained there until the following Friday when she slipped and made for Nassau. On Monday 10 January the British ship arrived at Nassau and welcomed onboard His Excellency the Governor of Bahamas. The Governor toured the ship for a couple of hours around lunchtime. Once the series of high profile VIP visits had been completed the cruiser was thrown open to local residents of Nassau and many hundreds toured the ship.

On Friday 14 January ***Superb*** sailed onto Kingston Jamaica, where after a weekend at sea she arrived on Monday morning and secured alongside the Trinidad Leasehold Oiling Jetty. ***Superb*** remained alongside for the next five days until sailing for the Panama Canal at Callao. After transiting the Canal she crossed the Equator at 08.15 on Tuesday 25 January. King Neptune and his court made an appearance onboard and punished all defaulters. Whilst working her way down the coastline of Chile, ***Superb*** paid courtesy visits to Valparaiso before arriving at the Falkland Islands on 20 February 1955. Leaving the Falklands on 24 February she sailed up the East Coast of South America. 9 March 1955 ***Superb*** was at Santos in Brazil and during that evening the ships band gave a most successful concert at the IV Centenary Exhibition Grounds in Sao Paulo. The performance being televised and filmed. Monday 14 March 1955 at 08.00 ***Superb*** arrived off Punta Santa Cruz and embarked pilot and liaison officers for Commodore and Wardroom. ***Superb*** fired a National Salute off Ilia de Villegagnon which was returned from Iiha da enxadas. ***Superb*** fired a salute to Admiral Commanding High Seas Forces flying his flag in the cruiser ***Barroso*** lying at a buoy off the naval base. Vice Admiral Sir John Stevens, KBE,

CB flying his flag in *Superb* arrived in Rio on 14 March on an official visit which ended on 21st March. Owing to dredging in the naval dockyard, arrangements had been made for *Superb* to berth in the deep-water dock, which lies at the foot of the Avenida Rio Branco.

Superb arrived at Bermuda on 15 April. She arrived at Bermuda in April having completed a very successful cruise in South America and some of the West Indian Islands. Whilst in Bermuda the crew took part in a very successful sports day held on Moresby Plain, *Superb* carried away most of the prizes. In the fleet regatta *Superb* was Cock of the Fleet.

Superb slipped from HM Dockyard Bermuda at 11.00 on Monday 20 June 1955 with all the main machinery in use. At 11.35 approximately 10 minutes after passing through the breakwater a considerable roaring noise followed by a loud and rapid knocking was heard in the after engine room from the vicinity of the starboard inner main circulator. The starboard inner ahead throttle was shut and after tripping the circulator the noise stopped. One minute later the forward engine room reported a heavy noise from the starboard outer main circulator, which was ordered to be stopped and then re-started.

Superb sailed from Bermuda and again transited the Panama Canal and visited ports on the West Coast of America and Canada.

On 24 June *Superb* arrived at Kingston Jamaica where she took on fuel and left later in the afternoon. Two days later she passed through the Panama Canal. By 3 July *Superb* had arrived off the wide natural harbour at San Diego home to the United States Navy. At San Diego seven hours of the six-day visit was spent in dry dock to clear *Superb's* air intakes.

Then it was onto the delights of San Francisco where the cruiser arrived on 18 July. As she approached the harbour entrance there was a dense fog bank that prevented views of San Francisco. When she went alongside the crew were stunned by the 15,000 private invitations that were received by the ship from the people of San Francisco. On the way out of San Francisco the crew got a great view of the Golden Gate Bridge. *Superb* left San Francisco with great memories on 20 July and continued her voyage northwards to Portland in Oregon.

On 23 July *Superb* arrived at Portland after a 87-mile journey up the Columbia River and another 13 miles up the Willamette river, going under bridges which seemed to be raised only inches above the truck. She moored in the centre of Portland, six feet away from a busy six-lane highway and beyond that the town. After five days she sailed onto Seattle in Washington State. *Superb* arrived on 29 July after an overnight passage for Seattle for Sea Fair Week and Beauty Queens, majorettes, can can girls and local VIP's.

The British cruiser left port on 4 August 1955 and headed across Puget Sound to call on the Canadian's at Vancouver. *Superb* remained in port for the next seven days before she sailed onto the Canadian Naval Base at Esquimalt. The British challenged the Canadians in a regatta and won all the trophies.

Superb sailed on 18 August and started her return journey to Bermuda, calling at Long Beach in California on 22 August for a six-day stay. The various attractions in Los Angeles meant that the crew was well entertained during the stopover. Her next port of call was Acapulco in Mexico, followed by an overnight transit of the Panama Canal on the night of the 12/13 September.

The cruiser's fuel tanks were topped up during a brief stop at Kingston in Jamaica on 15 September and four days later *Superb* returned to her berth at Bermuda. She sailed from Bermuda on 24 September and returned to Sheerness on Thursday 6 October to unload her ammunition. The RFA *Teakol* offloaded *Superb's* oil. De-ammunitioning was completed in record time of one forenoon and in the afternoon, wives and children, relatives and friends were welcomed onboard *Superb*. The next day *Superb* made her way up the River Medway to Chatham, where she arrived at 2.45 and was taken in hand for a refit.

Superb re-commissioned at Chatham on 14 February 1956 with Captain Earl Cairns in command for the General Service Commission. *Superb's* destination was to head East of Suez for the first and last time. After trials in the English Channel Superb sailed for Portland on Sunday 4 March. At Portland the Asian stewards and laundry staff were embarked and *Superb* sailed from Plymouth on 6 March 1956 for the East Indies station via Malta and the Suez Canal.

International news reached the ship in the form of troubles in the Persian Gulf and *Superb* was accordingly ordered to Malta with the utmost despatch. The cruiser arrived on Tuesday 13 March and was quickly stored before sailing for Aden. After five days at sea and after passing through the Suez Canal Superb arrived at Aden on Sunday 18 March. The cruiser's fuel tanks were topped up and by midnight the cruiser was back at sea en-route to Bahrien.

On 21 March *Superb* secured at Sitra for more oil and the cruiser started a cruise of the Persian Gulf soon there after. Having spent late March in the hot, sweltering heat of the Persian Gulf *Superb's* crew were pleased to hear that she was no longer required in the region. She was ordered to proceed to Colombo where she entered dry-dock for three-days. 200 ratings from the ship got a chance to enjoy the rest camp HMS *Uva* at Diyatalawa for four days. The Commander in Chief Vice Admiral Sir Charles Norris came onboard and welcomed the ship to the station. *Superb* sailed overnight to Trincomalee arriving on Thursday 19 April and then back to the Persian Gulf on the following Saturday.

Superb ended up at Bahrain and spent ten days swinging around the hook before returning to Trincomalee on Saturday 12 May. At Trincomalee the next three weeks were spent enjoying sports, leisure time and *Superb's* concert party gave two performances in the fleet cinema of 'Laughter Ahoy'.

On 1 June *Superb* was at Trimcomalee preparing for her East African cruise, which started in earnest on Wednesday 6 June when she slipped from the harbour and set a course for Mombasa in Kenya. The following day she encountered a tropical storm during which visibility dropped rapidly until at one point visibility extended for only half a mile. On Sunday 10 June speed was reduced due to an emergency appendix operation in sick bay, when the doctor requested that the ship be steadied as much as possible.

On Tuesday 12 June *Superb* heading northwards crossed the line and King Neptune once again made a visit to *Superb* and her crew at 11 in the morning. With the ceremony over by mid afternoon *Superb* continued on her course for Mombasa, where she eventually arrived on the following Friday. After a weekend of official visits from diplomats and government officials, *Superb* was open to visitors on Monday. The next seven days were spent at Mombassa, which allowed members of the crew some shore leave. Some crewmembers ventured into Kenya's national parks to experience some of the exotic and dangerous wildlife present there, others chose to experience the more simple pleasures of some glorious beaches on Kenya's coastline.

On Monday 25 June 1956 ***Superb*** sailed from Mombassa and headed towards Zanzibar with an arrival planned for early the following morning. At 08.00 on Tuesday 26 June ***Superb*** arrived off shore and fired a 21-gun salute. Later in the stay Superb was once again opened to visitors who toured the cruiser.

Superb left the British colony on Thursday 28 June and headed to Dar Es Salaam, where she arrived the following day.

On Sunday 1 July ***Superb*** was at Sar Es Salaam where the ship was open to visitors. The following day His Excellency the Governor of Tanganyika visited the ship. Two days later another VIP visited the ship. The Commissar for Rhodesia and Nyasaland was entertained onboard the ship and ***Superb*** was again opened to the public. The following Friday she sailed from Dar Es Salaam for Mombassa. At the Kenyan port ***Superb*** made a brief stop before continuing her journey to the tropical paradise islands that comprise the Seychelles in the middle of the Indian Ocean. The Capital of the thousand odd island chain is Male, and ***Superb*** anchored off the town on Wednesday 11 July. Hundreds of local boats brought a great many locals out to the ship and these were treated to tours of the cruiser on the following Friday.

Superb remained at Male until Tuesday 17 July when she sailed for Trincomalee. After five uneventful days at sea the British cruiser arrived at the wide-open harbour on the island. The area was full of other naval vessels preparing for a series of naval exercises in which Superb would fully participate. On Tuesday 31 July 1956 Vice Admiral Biggs boarded ***Superb*** at the start of the exercises in the waters around Trincomalee that continued until the middle of October.

HMS ***Superb*** left Trincomalee at midday on 20 October 1956. Indian warships operating in the area reported sighting some uncharted reefs. ***Superb*** being better equipped to map these was sent to investigate. Upon arriving at the given co-ordinates ***Superb*** found no reefs but did discover a large pod of whales.

After seven days at sea ***Superb*** reached land at 08.00 on 27 October when a Bahrain light vessel was sighted. ***Superb*** took on extra fuel before shifting berth to the Sitra anchorage.

The Suez Crisis on the opposite end of the Red Sea meant that the ship's arrival was a low-key affair and no formal ports of call were made. ***Superb*** left port quietly on 31 October at 04.10 in the morning and proceeded to Dubai at a speed of 27 knots.

Four days later ***Superb*** anchored off Dubai at 15.20. An-hour later three dhows came alongside the ship loaded with 160 officers and men of the First Battalion of the Gloucestershire Regiment. After many hours of transporting men and equipment to the cruiser ***Superb*** weighed at 21.08 and worked up to 27 knots.

Despite the cramped conditions onboard and the extra queues for the NAAFI stores no untoward incidents occurred on passage and ***Superb*** anchored about 40 miles to seaward of Mina El Armedi, out of sight of land at 15.00 on 1st November 1956. She remained at anchor until 7 November. A large deck sport programme was arranged to amuse the ships' company and soldiers during the dog-watches and film shows were increased. The ships concert party did extracts from their performances for the soldier's benefit.

On 7 November the ship sailed for Bahrain for fuel and provisions arriving on the night of 8th and sailing again at 19.00 the next evening to return to Mina anchorage. Whilst on passage the Imperial Iranian ***Babr, Palang*** and a small oiler and another vessel were observed anchored off Jaz Arabi.

At 08.30 on Monday 12 November ***Superb*** and the frigate ***Loch Insh*** weighed anchor and proceeded to sea for exercises in company. In the morning the close range and 4" guns were fired. In the afternoon ***Loch Insh*** came up on the starboard side of ***Superb*** and fired two half patterns of 3 Squids. Both ships anchored on completion of these manoeuvres at 17.30 in a position some way away from the original anchorage in the hope that the fishing might be better.

The two British warships sailed on the afternoon of 14 November for Bahrain at economical speed and proceeded alongside to fuel and to disembark the troops and their stores. The soldiers having left the ship ***Superb*** anchored at Sitra in the afternoon.

Superb remained at Sitra until 12 December except for local sea exercises with ***Loch Fyne, Loch Insh*** and ***Loch Killisport***. During this period HMS ***Jawada,*** a LCT on loan to the Qatar Petroleum Company was commissioned as a tender to ***Superb***.

On 12 December ***Superb*** having taken on fuel and embarked Tactical Headquarters 24th Infantry Brigade, Tactical Headquarters and two companies of the 1st Kings Shropshire Light Infantry and sailed at 20.00 for Sir Abu Nu'Air island. HM Ships ***Loch Fyne, Loch Killisport*** and ***Jawada*** had sailed in advance with the remaining two companies of the 1st Kings and vehicles.

The landing exercises had been, carried out by the frigates and ***Jawada*** on 12 December with ***Superb*** joining at daylight on 13th and full-scale exercises with air support were carried out throughout that day. It had been intended to carry out a final exercise at dawn on 14 December, but this was cancelled owing to unsuitable weather and the loss of ***Jawada's*** stern anchor. All the ships returned to Bahrain on completion of 'Shop Window' at dusk on 13 December. ***Superb*** meanwhile arrived at Sitra at 07.00 14 December and started the process of disembarking the troops.

Three days later the cruiser sailed for Khor Kuwai arriving at 11.00 the following day. ***Superb*** remained in Bahrain until 21 December when another landing exercise with Royal Marine Commandos took place. The exercise culminated in an operation to round up 20 'acting guerrilla's' who suitably clothed had been smuggled onto the island at dawn.

Superb returned to Bahrain arriving at 06.30 on 22nd December and remained alongside over the festive period. 1957 started at 11.00 when ***Superb*** sailed for Jazirat Sir Abu Nu'Air to carry out further landing exercises in company with ***Jawada***. ***Superb*** remained at Bahrain until 21 January undertaking repairs before heading onto Simonstown in South Africa.

On 12 February 1957 ***Superb*** sailed from Simonstown for the United Kingdom, calling at Freetown and Dakar on passage. Upon her arrival at Chatham on 4 March

Superb was taken into dockyard care for repairs and defects to be corrected and at the end of May she had joined the Home Fleet as Flagship of Flag Officer Flotilla's Home Fleet.

In Late May 1957 ***Superb*** was at Invergordon for Operation ***Steadfast,*** a Royal Review of the Home Fleet. Also in attendance were the carrier's ***Ark Royal, Ocean, Albion*** and the cruiser ***Gambia.*** During the days leading up to the Review the fleet rehearsed for the Royal Steam Past. The Royal Review occurred on Monday 27 May with ***Britannia*** taking the Royal party along the line of ships.

On 19 June ***Superb*** arrived at the Netherlands Naval Base at Den Helder, which was followed four days later by a transit of the Kiel Canal to arrive at Karlskrona in Sweden on 25 June. The British warship remained in port until 1 July when she sailed to take part in the five-day naval exercise Exercise ***Fairwind II*** in the North Sea. At the conclusion of this exercise, ***Superb*** returned to Rosyth for five days. Her final tour of ports would take in those with which ***Superb*** had associations and on 12 July the first of these was Shotley, where she remained for three days. On 16 July ***Superb*** sailed through the Solent and arrived at Portsmouth on her farewell cruise. Two days were spent at Portsmouth before she sailed the short distance to the other end of the Solent and anchored off Bournemouth for five-days from 18 July. At the end of this visit, ***Superb*** turned around and sailed up the English Channel towards Chatham, where she arrived for the final time on 24 July.

Over the weekend of 3/4/5 August 1957 ***Superb*** was open to the public at Chatham for Chatham Navy Days to her stern were the destroyers ***Alamein*** and ***Reward.*** This proved to be one of the last public appearances of the great cruiser as later in the month she was paid off and on 20 September the ship's company left the ship for the last time and were accommodated at Royal Naval Barracks at Chatham. ***Superb*** soon afterwards was placed into reserve at the Kentish Naval Base. ***Superb*** paid off in a ceremony at Chatham and was reduced to reserve. An opportunity to store the cruiser at Gareloch, alongside half sister ship ***Swiftsure*** was agreed and ***Superb*** was taken to Scotland. ***Superb*** would remain at Gareloch until she was declared surplus to requirements and sold for scrapping.

The cruiser eventually arrived under tow at the scrapyard of Arnott Young at Dalmuir on 8 August 1960 for breaking up to start. Once the scrap man had cut away enough, the hull of the once proud cruiser was towed to Troon where by 1961 ***Superb*** was cut into pieces and eventually disappeared.

SUPERB BATTLE HONOURS

PASSERO 1718

SADRAS 1782

PROVIDIEN 1782

NEGAPATAM 1782

TRINCOMALEE 1782

GUT OF GIBRALTAR 1801

SAN DOMINGO 1806

ALGIERS 1816

ALEXANDRIA 1882

JUTLAND 1916

STATISTICS

Ordered as part of the 1941 Supplementary Programme as part of the Tiger class. In 1945 Superb was allocated to the Swiftsure class.

Displacement:	Light 9066 tons
	Deep 11,564 tons
After 1950	Deep 11,851 tons
Dimensions:-	538 feet (pp)
	555.6 (oa)
	Beam 64 feet
Armament:-	Nine 6-inch MkXXIII on 3 triple Mk XXIII mountings (200rpg)
	Ten 4-inch Mk XVI on five twin Mk XIX mountings (200rpg)
	16 2pdr guns on four quadruple Mk VII mountings (1,800rpg)
	8 40mm Bofors
	2 20mm on single mountings
	2 20mm on twin mountings (hand worked)
	2 2pdr guns on single mountings
Armour	Turret roofs:- 2inches
	Sides of magazines: - 3.5 inches
	Sides of engine rooms: - 3.25 inches
Machinery	Parsons geared turbines, 4 shafts, 80,000 ship. Speed 32.25 knots
Fuel capacity	1,700 tons
Complement:	733 (peacetime), 900 war.

SUPERB'S COMMANDING OFFICERS

Captain W G A Robson DSO DSC	21 August 1945
Captain R M T Taylor DSC	15 April 1947
Captain A K Scott-Moncrieff DSO	21 December 1948
Captain Sir Anthony W Buzzard DSO OBE	4 January 1950
Captain W J Yendell	1 November 1950
Captain E W J Bankes	16 May 1951
Commodore R Tosswill OBE	30 September 1952
Commodore D H Connell-Fuller	9 April 1954
Captain Earl Cairns	14 December 1955
Lieutenant Commander K Bannar-Martin DSC	1. February 1958

INDEX

D

E

T

U

V